REFLECTION OF LIFE

AN ANTHOLOGY OF POEMS
VOLUME II

RAMESH CHANDRA PRADHANI

Dedicated to all the poetry lovers

Who stimulate me forever

To ink somelines quite inspiring

Who really love what I wish to express

Spontaneously with the Almighty's grace.

My heartfelt gratefulness to one and all

Who like and dislike my thoughts and emotions, after all.

Ramesh Chandra Pradhani

Contents

Contents

Contents

Contents

Contents

Foreword

Life is the amalgam of elation and melancholy,ups and downs, victory and defeat, success and failure and above all it is the blend of light and darkness. Here the brave and the confident lots can explore the dual aspects and get encouraged by the positive vibes shunning the negative ones.The fact is that the confident and optimistic people strive hard to search light in darkness and failure,fear or disappointment can never shake their identity. Often the force of the strong will is found among the geniuses all around us , in the great works of the luminaries and also in the thoughts engraved in the bosom of the poems, stories, essays,biographies,travelogues etc. And I see the excellent literary creation 'Reflection of Life' by my dear friend Ramesh Chandra Pradhani is a nice platform to expose the ideas noble and inspring. Really my friend's high spirit behind the publication deserves immense praise. Moreover his determination, persistent hard work and confidence has enabled him to reach such a height of glorious achievement. I am sure the novelty inculcated in the anthology might move the readers to regard this work as the worthy asset.

Durbadal Ghibela
Reader in English
Jarasingha College,Jarasingha
Dist. Balangir (Odisha)

Preface

Life is full of huddles.It does not mean that it can not be overcome. Without ups and downs, no life exists to grow and move on. Nevertheless, life is not easy, we can make it easy by following something that really enriches life with divine spirit as well as the teaching imparted by mistakes and righteousness. Future life can be reshaped by means of enjoying and speculating the present we live in. What we do or think at present certainly nurtures our destiny. Something inspiring or somebody helpful, friendly and accommodating always deserve to be taken up. The present anthology of poetry, Volume-V, that is, the REFLECTION OF LIFE is the reservoir of inspirationnal thoughts and enlightenment. Moving is the heart of this anthology to take one into the world of hope, faith and confidence.

I am sure this anthology will serve as the guiding star on the path of the journey to the destination. Further, it rejoices life in a unique way to sustain humanity, peace, love and happiness.

Ramesh Chandra Pradhani

Acknowledgements

Thoughts, emotions, feelings are conspicously reflected in the present book of poetry anthology "THE REFLECTION OF LIFE" along with internal and external circumstances and various situations experiencing in life dealing with all shades of life- love and anger success and failure etc. Though the book is the outcome of my vehement efforts and enthusiasm, it would not be possible without some helping hands and their whole hearted moral support.

At the very outset, my heartfelt gratitude to the whole team of Notion Press for their generosity and commitment in bringing out the anthology of poetry, THE REFLECTION OF LIFE in time.

My humble gratefulness to my friend Durbadal Ghivela, Reader in English, Jarasingha College, Jarasingha who always extend his magnanimous hands heartily and devote his valuable time and labour for the publication of the anthology.

Hearty thanks to Bimal Kathar, one of my employees who incessantly support me in all respect in preparing the manuscript of the anthology.

Last but not the least, I am also thankful to my betterhalf, son and daughters for their encouragement and stimulation in publishing a book on poetry anthology like "THE REFLECTION OF LIFE."

Ramesh Chandra Pradhani

Prologue

"The REFLECTION OF LIFE", an anthology of poems, Volume-V
    Is the veridical reflection of my life moving around where I live
    And garnering from here and there which I wish to leave
    On the sands of time through the REFLECTION OF LIFE
    Earnestly I hope, each poem will wash away human stife.
    This is a collection of one hundred and ten poems in all
    Each one, more or less, depicts something someway
    Touching the symphony of human feelings-rise and fall
    Love and hate, beauty and ugliness, war and peace
    In reality both are the sourcess of divine bliss
    Which can, together build humans future edifice.

Ramesh Chandra Pradhani

1. CORUSCATION

Friend of truthfulness always a man of coruscation
Friends of thankfulness draw everyone's attention.
Friends of kindness sway in brightness
Friends are friends who never hide weakness.
Friends of forgiveness epitome of godliness
Friends replete with sacredness.
Friends of magnanimity mountainous in adversity
Friends show the light of equality and equity.
Friends of openness and frankness win the hearts of multitudes
Friends of sameness never show attitudes.

2. NEW CREATION

Creation something new
Occurs on the ruin of a few
Timely actions save many
Out of its cruelty and tyranny.
Some creation may be renewed
Reshaping the existing avenue.
Imitation sometimes brings recreation
Recreation does not mean imitation
Both creation and recreation needs imagination
As primary and secondary in definition.
Newness of creation emerges
When the old ones quite perishes
Compulsion of curiosity in mind gushes
Something often behind pushes.
Heart breaks, anguish makes into pieces
Then and there unique creation rushes.
Destruction fives birth to noble creation
Construction on the passage of time falls into devastation.

3. LIFE A MATTER OF BALANCE

Life has two sides of the same coin

In the absence of one the other is vain.

When life a mixture of pain and pleasure

Leaving one how can measure.

Life is river flowing forward to end

Having two shores aside to remain.

Day and night only makes a day to name

Day without night or night without day cannot pass on.

Life a matter of balance to survive

Sometimes for existence revolt and revive.

Life an amalgam of light and darkness

Amidst gregariousness and loneliness.

Life begins where it ends to make a cycle of process

Birth and death inevitable and certain to progress.

4. FROZEN

When words are frozen mouth suffers
When wages, behavior differs
Some moments stop moving
Time hampers in nature's growing
But when heart frozen emotions and feelings pile
Cheerlessly start groaning
Tears cannot wash away dullness of life
As colours defile itself
Pleasure ready to exile in the forest of own profile
As frozen forest unable to exhale
Nor it can inhale
Life grapples to survive in the midst of hallucinations.

5. LOVE

Love unites the unknown, the unseen of two souls
Absence of love in one can paralyze the whole
Love is the understanding of place, person and action.
Misunderstanding breaks the bond of closeness and affection.
Love is a means of sharing each other
Without love life becomes the lifeless creature.
Love is action not words to flatter
No love, no life can glitter
Love is light to show the path in the dark of life
Anger of love invites the human strife
Love is a flicker of hope to live with humanity
Lack of love can demolish the edifice of society
Love is strength to stand for the justice and righteousness
Excess love lets one go astray with nothingness.
Love is the cause of both construction and destruction
Fall and rise, ups and downs, promotion and degradation.
Love is amalgam of lies and truth, risk and safety
Silence and communication, simplicity and complexity
More is lost, more is ruined, and more is regained
Love comes out of the pit of anger, envy and hatred.

6. POWER OF SILENCE

Echoed beyond the horizon
Earth to heaven
Surpassing the great walls
Of forest and mountain
Enters into the heart of everyone.
More faster than mobile network
No need of multi tower
No need of any thin wire
Itself the unseen connective.
No storm, cyclone tornado, tempest in any form
Prevents the connection between sender and receiver
Makes them so closer.
Vigorous is the sound of silence.

7. TESTIMONY

Mother needs no testimony to take care of children
To love, nurture, rear without any condition
Can a tree require to give away flowers and fruits?
Can the sun need anybody's to enlighten?
Everyone has a purpose to serve
Destined to deserve something to preserve
We are not for us but for others
Who even share and care forever
Testimony arises where doubts dominates
Humanity lost and humans go astray
No power under the sun can change
Unless and until we change ourselves.

8. LITERACY LIBERATES SOUL

Not just recognition of letters
Means not only writing or reading
Literacy Liberates human soul
From the bondages of problems or fouls.
Literacy makes one understand
Oneself and near and dear ones in narrow sense
Broadly it enables to explore the world around us
Stops people deceiving one another
Let's fight for literacy for us together
And help the nation dreaming bright future.
Literacy checks and balances the error committed
Corruption, suppression, operations out rooted
Consciousness raises its head without any coyness
Malafide intention sinks deep under the alertness.

9. I HAVE A DREAM

Some dream I have I wish come true
A society where both man and woman equally blessed
With the same grace of Almighty, so no hatred
Where let old helpless parents be worshipped.
Where no betrayal in love, words or action
Where no corruption, no exploitation or no molestation
Let the buds bloom without any spoliation
Where live the gods and goddesses in diverse incarnation.
Let humans travel on the highway of positivity
Explore the world to search the best of fertility
Understand oneself and others with the perception of maturity
Let things grow in their own way to pluck the fruits of humanity.
Dreaming a realm of peace and prosperity
Where people are devoid of anger, envy and enmity
Far from the madding crowd of selfishness and gravity
Spreading the fragrance of equality, justice and fraternity.
Dreaming a heart replete with symphony of feelings
A heart open and frank for all with cheers and smiling
A mind with broad and heightened sensibility.

10. PASSION

Passion makes a man creative
Hardly can adversity find defective.
Passion makes a man positive
Enables those active in better perspective.
Passion makes a man constructive
Proves one's dynamic and enthusiastic motif.
Passion makes a man different
Placing in the place of achievement.
Passion enriches mind to fruitfulness
Healing the ailments of loneliness.

11. RESPECT

Respect to get respect without any suspect

Respect being bodyguard always wholeheartedly protect.

Respect to win the anxious hearts of multitudes

Respect can change negative to positive attitudes.

Respect yourself to calm down your ego and anger

Respect undoubtedly spares you from inevitable danger

Respect respecting women in the society

Respect can do away with women atrocity.

Respect one to respect one further and further

Respect will make chain to bind all in relation together.

12. A YEAR OF RESTORATION

Let the New Year be a year of restoration
What we have left in isolation
Let it fulfill its ambitions amidst commotions
Respect with due regards to women
The backbone of not only the family but also a nation
Whose presence makes the world a beautiful heaven?
Whose caring and nursing enliven life?
With the rhapsody of soul's compassion
Towards the sustenance of love harmony and union..
Let fraternity reside in the heart of mankind
As an identity exclusively distinct
Let people not forget their instinct.
Let the New Year come with a new beginning
With much hope, faith and confidence dreaming
To cooperate one and all towards the progress aspiring
Being the lamp post on the way to victory stand smiling
Leaving the intense pain and suffering behind
Let's learn how to march forward to survive
The best of the past may kindly be revived
The epitome of commonsense and knowledge however mournful.

13. TIME IS POWERFUL

• 13 •

For time changes everything
Spares nobody or nothing
Time brings chilly winter to ruin
So does spring, newness to coin
With the passing of time runs the rivulet
Widened the river and vast sea to accommodate
Dark clouds to clean the cerulean sky
Transparent the scene, the sun rises high.
Men of penury can rise to the gallery of opulence
Houseful of confluence, sure to vacate in silence.

14. TRY AGAIN BETTER

Nobody is perfect from his birth
Nothing is perfect from its creation
It is the efforts that make one able
It is the revisions that make something possible
Loser is he who does not try again
Incessant Endeavour can solve any problem
Continuous falling of water on a piece of stone
Makes it soften to break into pieces
Regular walking on foot unleashes green grass or bush
A clean way is formed on the passage of time.
Trying again and again enables to defeat
What cannot be done only once be possible in repeat.

15. TAKE ME BACK

Take me back to those golden moments
When passed time
With life full of merriment
Where no criticality or conspiracy
Where no pretention or secrecy.
Take me back to those companions
Who considered me one of the champions?
Who unconditionally came out to help me?
Still in search of those times, forget how can I?
Take me back to those places
Where no tension, no losses
Where no rivalry, no worries
Only freedom of expression, no enemies.

16. LIFE IS BOOK

We are all readers
Life being a book
Having so many chapters
Daily read a chapter
To swallow the matter.
Reading is a necessity
Brings us fertility
Making creative and productive
Lay the foundation of life effective
Silently, slowly but steadily
Little by little but incessantly.
Some days it will show us
The right path with a purpose.

17. DON'T WAIT FOR SUCCESS

As water does not rush to the thirsty,

Rather the thirsty reach to the water in hasty

Success never comes to anybody silent

But everywhere in disguise present

It is seen to those who are diligent

Hard workers can pave the way to the success

Without waiting and dreaming in luxury and happiness

Better not to wait and watch to success

Do your duty with honesty and integrity for access.

18. LEADERS ARE READERS

Leaders to lead

Experience to feed

Amalgam of sacrifice and dedication

Daring personality to deal

Every situation to heal

Reader of the creation to read

Struggling hero to proceed.

Among all the skilled controller

Revered coordinator

Elegant motivator.

Real warrior to bring unity

Efficient worker of equality

Agile developer to positivity

Diligent and patient in identity

Evergreen, sharper and stronger

Reshapers, recreator and revitalizer.

19. WRITE TO BE READ

Writing for reading is obvious
We read what is written precious
Accept with confidence anxious
Attention and mind conscious.
Writing something glorious
What is right is the purpose
In all respect is punctilious
Makes readers studious.
Credence grows marvelous
Trust to rely tremendous
Follow compulsion conscientious
Matter hilarious and rigorous.
Writing with clarity and vivacity
Vivid and lucid in objectivity
More creative more creativity
Plead for understanding capacity.

20. A PRIVATE LIFE

• 20 •

Make your life private
Happiness to accumulate
Freedom to inculcate
Search within to locate.
Let not life to be suffocated
Under the blanket of public
Where no choice respected
Even though it is cosmic.

21. ROSES HAVE THEIR OWN BEAUTY

Roses thy name is beauty
Lovely creation of Almighty
Dedicated to other's self
A bridge between the two souls
Symbol of love, peace and unity.
Roses thy name is sanctity
Born for the creations entity
Lover's and love's identity
Teaches mankind solidarity.

22. BE KIND AND STAY SOFT

Kindness changes you to be the best
No sun of rage will burn your chest.
You can garner every power of God
Makes others laugh as blooming bud.
Kindness makes you soft and sober
To allure every mind for thy favour.
That flavour and fervor quite divine
Can build your destiny more sublime.

23. LET LIFE DO SOMETHING

Life is to live
To live is to do
To do is to share
To share is to care
Caring needs to be fair.
Life is to grow
To grow is to take time
Time changes every moment
Every moment a precious gift
Gift is to accept and respect unhurt
Knows not when changes come to lot.
Life is to flow
To flow is to move forward
Moving passes through cervices of ups and downs
To be the first to reach the goalpost.
The rest breaks the record of history.

24. YOU ARE NOT YOURS

As a child you belong to your parents
As a husband to your wife
As a father to your children
As a sufferer to your strife
You are not yours, you cannot deny.
It is not yours what you earn
It is not yours what you learn
For you, you are not born
You come as it is your turn.
Your body is not yours
It is for someone to look
Your mind is not yours
It is for someone to hook.
Your hand is not yours
It is for someone to help
Your leg is not yours
It is for someone to delve.
Your heart is not yours
It is for someone if meant
Your emotions are not yours
It is for someone to vent.
Your words are not yours
Either for someone to please
Or for someone to tease.
Think in which you are at ease.

Your life is not yours
It is someone's kindness
Why then selfishness
How long its existence?
You are not yours, my dear
Let yourself be endeared
In no way there will be fear
Till you live, practice to cheer.

25. RICH MAN

Really rich is he
Who bears an open heart?
As tender as flower
During the time of pleasure
As hard as coconut
In adventure or danger.
Who possess constructive mind
Where no place of conspiracy
No pretention, no irritation
No priority of exploitation
Emulating own relation
No desire of manipulation
For the sake of own generation.
Who has no boundary of jealousy?
No enemy of short temper
An empire less emperor
Weapons less soldier
Worldwide humanity conqueror.

26. DECEMBER COLDEST YET SWEETEST

Last but not the least in attraction

Coldest enough to seek warmth of affection.

A time of togetherness to remind reminiscences

All around the merry mood of fun and fest beyond the fences.

More joyful to greet the new in as every time

More doleful to depart the old out sometime.

Leaving some footprints takes a sojourn to replace

Worldwide nature's call profoundly embraces to grace.

Universal lore it imparts with rejuvenation to mankind

A reason is there seen or unseen but felt behind.

Every living plant or animal destined to decay with a passage of time

No matters or materials lasts long perpetually sublime.

Color fades, age counts down, white turns grey charmless

Green leaves to yellow, dry and fall to the ground helpless.

27. BE WHAT YOU ARE

If you compare with others, you will be your enemy
You start fighting with you, mind with soul
Things fall apart with drastic change
Love to hatred and betrayal
Relation to exploitation
Dedication to manipulation
Loyalty, integrity to conspiracy
Humanity replaced by brutality.
By comparing you sow the seeds of jealousy
That consumes you day by day
You can never escape from lunacy
The loss you can't repay.
Be what you are to stay in peace
You is yours never try to miss.

28. UNDERWHELM

Sweet words never comes out in anger
Users of rough language are sentiment monger
Who blindly passes comments more sharper?
Than the edge of a knife that may cut own finger.
Distance makes a gap of understanding
Carefree, tension free in thinking and doing
Bad or good not at all a matter of introspecting
The consequence of what one wishes.
Near and dear, bosom friends even family underwhelmed
By negativity, monopoly and excess haughtiness dwelled
Actions or reactions congenial to ambience always suits
No disappointments engulf but let anyone to pluck the fruits.
Silence instead often allures for the quest of novelty
Leave not others be underwhelmed by your ingenuity
Better to remain away from superficiality
The reason of mistaken embellishment in purity.

29. WHEN THOU ARE MINE

In the empyrean of my mind even in gelid snow
Thou are the silvery moon
Stars twinkle in thy shine to croon
Stilly mead underneath starts swaying soon.
Roaming in the dingle in your presence
Makes me feel what you are in essence
Unforgettable but unbearable the moment staying afar
Your absence turns me a lifeless log bar.
Needless to say how things happen quiet
But always I long for the right
When saw you at first sight
Since you become my super might.

30. PEACE

Argue not with nonsense talking
Compare not with others for emulating
No sound sleep be stolen away
When you are on your own way.
The more you take, more you feel headache
More expectations, more tension to rack
Less desire, less affairs least concern
Road closed for the surge of consternation.
Be the extinguisher to douse the fire of desire
Be the clouds of your own to quench the thirst of being millionaire
Only you are the anchor of your uncertain future
When you can laugh heartily you can conquer rapture.
Living in arena of nothingness opens the gate of peace
Be what you are wondrously provides bliss
Soaring high in search of luxury pushes you down
The rest depends upon you to be crowned as monarch of throne.

31. JUMP FOR JOY

Life is a matter of merriment, joy and smile
Unwise to keeping oneself away from miles
Be careful life is Almighty's gift
Forever tries to rejoin the rift
Avoid not, never ever lose and think unfit.
Never take the load of strain and stress
Free yourself from bondage of depression, refresh
Be positive and sanguine of His grace
Every wound and ailments it will dress.
Incorporate in you all what necessitates
Dare to forget those what never associates
Life will absolutely be yours to jump and joy
Time is not for waste but to fairly enjoy.

32. KARMA

First and foremost dharma (religion) of humans is karma (duty)

Small or big no matter Kala (art) is karma.

Karma teaches how to survive

Feed us, nourishes us to revive.

Karma is the choice to obtain

Humanity in the society to sustain.

Karma is the option in both selection and election

It is potion, protection,, construction for generations.

Karma is hope, life and light to live with purpose

Karma is the panacea to all evils in cosmos.

Karma makes man active to dream the golden future

Love it, hug it mingle with it to wholly nurture.

Karma is truth, knowledge and wisdom

Sing the hymns of karma to release boredom.

Karma is perfection, karma is fulfillment

Sows the seeds of compromise and adjustment.

33. LIFE'S MANY JOURNEYS

Where there's life, there's journey to take
Life's many journeys in the same way make.
No beginning no end of life's journey
Either passes through the road rosy or thorny.
Many a restless journey reaches the goal
Crooning in silence the rhapsody of the soul.
Journey accompanied by a fearless mind of resolutions
Can break multiple chains of hallucinations
The path of journey no longer long and unreached
When taken with a purpose and target to achieve.
Life journey start with a baby of helplessness
Life sways in the cradle of mother's kindness
Merrymaking the childhood journey with pamper
In the midst of several fugitive temper
The youth the mid journey resolves many promises
Curiosity and inquisitiveness enables to accomplishes
Manhood journey of life like the setting sun
Tearing the blanket of clouds and fog ahead run
Resting in the lap from where it emerges
Just refresh to reappear in a new form, new images.

34. BEYOND THE HORIZON

Resplendent scenic beauty of nature marvels

When alluring hues of setting sun start glowing behind the horizon

Cerulean sky bathes in the golden pool of loneliness

Kissing the mountain stiff in love with brightness

Make the depressed soul brush off its filth of unconsciousness.

When man of greediness becomes solitary in confinement

Seeks the shelter of nature gazing at the remotest sight

Previously preoccupied mind twirls in the whirl of nature to alleviate appetite

Mind in consolation runs away from far from the madding crowd of selfishness

Dreaming of touching and robbing the wondrous seductress in steady silence.

The oppressed life, abandoned by the near and dear, remembers the sanctity of nature's generosity

As if wished to breathe his last in the lap of a serene nature of purity.

Heart then starts trilling in magnificent amusement unforgettable

Rhapsody of soul buzzing in the whisper randomly chooses attachment impeccable.

Beyond the horizon either in the sunset or sunrise a stream of stimulation

A flicker of faith and confidence keeps enlightening deserted population

More amazing the glazing sun appears to be vermilion on the forehead
of a beauty
Mesmerizes the lookers on sight to stealthily tap the finger on red spot
so pretty.

35. HAPPY REPUBLIC DAY, 2022

Happy Republic Day to all my country fellow, respect to pay

Humble honour to the constitution of India came into force on this day

Among the people of the whole India engraved in red letter today

People of India felt happy to have a nation of self administration

People governed by own people's representatives

Yet to receive better and fair administration.

Rights are many to enjoy

Equality the essence of humanity

Peace the ultimate weapon to acquire

Unity the soul of human's life

Benevolence to the whole mankind

Loyalty liberates the soul to take responsibility

Integrity creates universal identity

Change provides opportunities to dream of perfection.

Day of celebration to remember the significance of constitution

Added with several amendments for smooth running of nation

Yesterdays of time reminds not to forget the beginning.

36. LITERATURE

Lighthouse for the sea voyagers to show the path of voyage

Inspiration for deriving pleasure and knowledge

Talisman to drive away disappointment and bondage

Enlightenment of mind, heart body and soul taking mileage

Reflection of life to rectify mistakes and beautify ugliness

Announces poetic justice- punishment for the culprit and justice to righteousness

Tells the story of both the vice and virtue, pain and pleasure

Universality and permanence the essence of literature

Records the history of past and present for the convenience of future

Enthusiasm, entertainment and everlasting wealth of society, culture.

37. ANTICIPATION

Each life is made up of anticipation
Life moves on the wheel of expectations.
Grand total depends on calculation
Wise are those who know before prediction.
Clear expression emerges out of prior indication
A prudent step to save something from ruination.
Understanding of inevitable situation
Sometimes makes one avoid with cunning perception.
Anticipation cent percent provides right actions.
Comp rending the world of hallucinations.
It makes one read what may happen next
Labor and time over the action does not go waste.
Men of anticipation are men fetching solutions
They themselves are solutions to some problems of confrontation.
Large heartedness getting rid of negative attitude
Broad mindedness plays the game of critical aptitude
Anticipation galvanize one for worldwide participation
With the highest culmination of lifelong ambition.
Men of anticipation are precursors of precautions
Their anticipation is just like doctor's prescriptions.

38. THE HAND THAT GIVES

The hand that gives is a true doner
The Almighty returns back sooner.
The hand that helps is real wealth
Saves many a life from death.
The hand that feeds is unending source
Showers from heaven in due course.
The hand that extends for betterment
Enriched with magnanimity and commitment.
The hand that bears the load of others
Is made with divine iron of strength.
The hand that treats the patient
Highly honored and recognized by the omnipresent.
The hand that washes away the filth of humanity
Sparkle like a diamond in reality.
The hand that writes the song of peace and happiness
God writes his name in the book of perpetuity and newness.

39. A JOURNEY TOWARDS IMMORTALITY

A singer- a divine artist, the queen of mellifluous voice

The Nightingale of India no more to rejoice

Her journey has just started mortality to immortality

Resting a sojourn in the abode of divinity.

Her name entwined the hearts of the whole mankind

Leaving an impeccable and sempiternal trace behind

Will be the perennial source of inspiration even in her absence

Enlightening the world of music, song and melody the life's essence.

No adieu, thou are in the mind and heart of one and all

As long as the world exists, indestructible your soul.

She was not a woman but a superwoman, a real heroine

Moon among the stars to sparkle and the realm of songs to shine.

40. BE

Be kind to one and all
Everybody will raise you before you fall
The footprints left definitely recall.
Be fair in dealings, must you prefer
Without feelings of a rapper
Everyone will revere and refer
Be the last option, nothing will defer.
Be honest in words
Echoes of your voice fast to touch the heart
Before one thinks of a start.
Be true to what you are
Nobody is there to tar
Before you does stand no bar.

41. DOING NO MISTAKES

Mistakes are not done rather happen unconscious
Some mistakes under subconscious are rigorous
But mistakes under conscious are sternly noxious
Embrace each mistake, a lesson too precious.
Mistakes are necessities to enrich each part of life
Consciousness of doing no mistakes
Is a great mistake to leave something incorrigible?
Wrong cannot be right unless and until comprehensible.
Man of no mistakes is likely to be omniscient or a lunatic
No person under the sun born with squeaky clean
Mistakes only pave the way, experience to glean
And experiences vouchsafe practical knowledge.

42. BETTER DAYS

Better days never come better for a hater
Days are neither sweet nor bitter in the language of a poetaster
It is our thoughts in which can shelter
Both are same if you filter or flatter in the voice of a songster
The way you see through gutter not always blotter.
Days are better only when battered on the anvil of a tester
Emerged through dust and moisture, mud and water
Enlightened by the thunderbolt and black clouds glitter
Whacked by the master blaster spinner or a batter.
Bitter days repeatedly test patience and diligence
Read your mind, nature, behavior and intelligence
Drench in the lake of torture, gloom and penitence
Making everything convenient for better day's resilience.
Better days come with the twittering of little birds
In the reconciliation of lovers with a resolute fresh start
Loving, caring and sharing each other by heart
Better days can never be apart.

43. HOME IS A PERSON

• 45 •

More than a person he takes heed

Saving from sun, rains and cold wind

Every morning he reminds to have a fresh start

Like a philosopher, argues smart

Never betrays, never hates whatever you

Houses in love, caring and sympathizing too.

Warmth in winter, coolness in summer

Dry and tender in rainy water.

No permission required to enter

Convinces the dipressed soul

Hailing coordially being a waitor

As readers are invited by a narrotar.

44. WHEN MOMENTS BECOME MEMORIES.

People become lessons when moments become memories
Passed time though comes back itself
Remains in core of heart on shelves
People associated with the moment leaves with lessons
However, in various places varies from persons to persons
Both the people and the moment, think not useless
Never ever dispel, digress or disgrace.
Life made up of so many memories
Offen works as calories
Stimulates to compose plenty of stories
Complied in the book of mankind
Some are deleted, some are edited
Some needs rectification to be glorified
Retaining the best to be incorporated.

45. DON'T BE PERFECT, BE REAL

Perfect needs more attention to the best

In haste doing something or making a waste

Perfect an imitation of something or somebody

May nit be true, lying in disguise muddy?

Decoration in one way seems perfect

But in other eyes looks imperfect

Changes take place many a time to be perfect

Still left half done in suspect.

No human is perfect and never be in future

Be real to near the perfection of culture

Which will provide you rapture

In the rest of life.

46. WE ARE JUST STRANGERS

Believe or not we are just strangers
Sometimes dangers often rangers
At any time disappear from the stage of life
Without taking anything with us to hive
To be near and dear is better than to be strangers
Always to display the masquerade of pleasures.
Strangers dont have any revengers
No place to occupy forever as managers
No possessons to handover one after the other.
We are just strangers no right to influence
Anybody or anything for power or greediness
As nothing or nobody remains in permanence.

47. EVERYTHING HAS LESSON

Everything has a lesson to teach
Learn and accept to be rich
In thoughts, ideas, actions and reactions
The best to be found with gratification
Big or small, high or low no matters
Everything has its value and character.
Everything has its own place and position
In their presence or absence when felt
Even a little bit of moment if we accept
Gives us the reservoir of precept
To make every life purposefull
As everything is meaningfull
Underestimate not the thing around us
Because everything has its own purpose.

48. A GOOD LIFE NEEDS SOME BAD DAYS

Lotus germinates from mud
Flowers come out from the dark of buds
Hot anger from cooling love and affection
Result sheet for grand total from addition
How can a good life be a subtraction?
From some bad days of convulsion.

49. LIFE IS COMING AND GOING

If you are born death is inevitable
Coming and going are unavoidable
Things come and go in perfect time
No time can stop or allow to move fine
Meeting myriads of people entwine
Relation, attachment ephemerally shines
Mourning is valueless when departing soul
Filling the gap is necessary as a whole.

50. DIE WITH MEMORIES, NOT DREAMS

Death will come one day, leaving all mourning
Coward is he who dies with dreams seeing
Before demise do some memorable
The whole will remain grateful
Do something innovating for wellbeing
After death life will sway in swing
Dreaming is good but making true is difficult
Leave this world with perpetual occult.

51. TRUST TAKES TIME AND TIME TAKES TRUST

Living being grows to stand still

Facing sun, rain, light to refill

Refinement comes after frequency of time

One comes when other goes if weather is fine

Time moves step by step to reach culmination

Dark is the reverse of light reflection

Seeing and hearing different from each other

Time and trust a matter of observation together.

52. COMPANIONSHIP

• 54 •

Cheerful is life when there's a jocund company
Replete with love, peace and harmony
Quite interesting traveling a long journey
With a companion of commitment no need of any testimony
True company never waits for time or money
What needed is a rapport of symphony.

53. CHANGE

Change is the law of Nature, we have to admit
None can stop the current of electricity
A massive mistake, we need not commit
Inevitable is the transition to balance diversity
Change is the process of revolt and revival
Making home a heaven for survival.

54. BE LIGHT

Be light to show the path in darkness
Be light to impart knowledge goodness
Be light to share your loneliness
To enrich the mind of sacredness
Be light to sacrifice for wellbeing of others
Be light to make others see the best together.
The world will choose you the best of all.

55. THE MAGIC OF SMILES

Smile is natural available free of cost
Life is lost if smile lost.
Smile is a tonic giving a feeling of vigor
Enliven everyone being a tranquillizer.
Smile a Brahma weapon to vanquish mighty power
A panacea to all social evils and bad hour.
Smile is human's alluring beauty
A smiling face can win chronic enmity.
Smile is real cosmetics looks so seductive
All negative attitudes turn to positive.
Keeps smiling talk smiling anywhere?
Be the centre of attraction everywhere.

56. REAL ONES STAY IN BAD TIMES

Bad time comes and goes
Still nobody wishes it
Nobody wants to stay in it
After seeing someone's, fleet
Leaving a cry of bleat
Such people betray thee
But real ones stay in bad times
Coz, they understand.

57. RIGHT PEOPLE

Right people do the best
Never anything in haste
Good deeds make them live
Even after the mundane world they leave
They stay in the heart of the time to come
No power under the sun can abandon.
Right people and right things are not easy
And easy people are not always right
Think before what you have to cite
Thus, you need not to excite.

60. EVERYTHING THAT YOU ARE ENOUGH

You are everything

You are male you are female

You are human you are animal

You are ugly you are beautiful

Everything is in you

You are anger you are peace

You are love you are hatred.

So many options you are

Choice is yours

And be the choice not the option.

60. FASCINATIONS

Women are all in all to have fascination to men for ages
Resplendent flowers of love captivate sages
Nature in serenity with mind-blowing beauty join broken heart
Rainbow in the azure sky enlivens from the core fast
But the character and personality of humans more impressive
When all others may be illusive and destructive.

61. SILENCE

A language of heart
Speaks a lot being smart
Understands the inner self
More worthy than any pelf
Solutions to every problem
By force never claims
Makes the mountain move
Silence itself a proof.

61. FOOTPRINTS

• 63 •

Short lived are the footprints on the sands of rivers
Deleted are they with the pressure of others
Or taken away by the naughty waves of water
Behind the waves are marked again footprints of sailors.
But the footprints of personality on the sands of time
For decades after decades leaving one's behind
Exists forever and reminds the stiffing past of mankind
To wake and warm up the slack generations from the core of heart and mind.

62. ENERGY

Surrender thyself to Him who loves you
Stick to your duty for the goodness to rescue
Energy will run through whole body to rise
Your mind and heart and save from fall.
Energy gleans from various sources
Not only from sumptuous food
But also from buoyant mood
Sometimes from pensive mood.
As life an amalgam of joy and sorrows
Both equally complementary to each other
Excess joy or sorrows can endure energy
For paving the way of sociology.
Dark side of life works as potion
When one dives in meditation
A doorway to the pristine salvation
Being the energy of introspection.
Everything may be a small or big source
If you embrace, it will be a force
Pushing you to the realm of creation
The last rests in sensation.

63. POSITIVE THOUGHTS

Positivity enriches the mind and heart with possibility

Like effective tonic increases potentiality

Positive thoughts come out of positive mind

Acclaiming the assurance of goodness for the mankind.

Lessen every dilemma and anxiety in silence

Assure hope and faith for convenience

Removing lingering impertinence

Mindset changes to accept all challenges.

Serve as the potion to body and mind

Energy provider enabling to march forward

Being positive makes one constructive

Can never allow anybody to be destructive.

Positive mind creates positive thoughts

Positive thoughts bring positive results

Positive results ensure sure success

Success is sum total of positive efforts.

64. EARTHDAY

Nurture Earth to nurture yourself
Care her to care you sound and safe
Love her; worship her by heart and soul
She will definitely shape your dole.
She is the mother, care taker and booster
Bears innumerable wealth forever
For her offspring to enjoy
On her lap a comfort zone incomparable
So ease and tender indescribable.
Have a promise on the earth day
To do something good every day
A little effort little by little incessant
Will make our other pregnant.
The best among the planets
In the universe the only habitat
Where life grows and satiates
All deficiency she can alleviate.
O plants and creatures let her breathe
Remain aloof from wheezing and stealth
Let her live for us to live, be blithe
The more you suffer, more you deceive.

65. EMPATHY

Great are those who understand others' feelings
Respect their sentiments smiling
Humans are those who share and care
Others in time of pain and pleasure being fair.
It works as a bridge between couples
Relation lasts long through the ripples
When caressed one's forehead joy multiples
None can, by force, the union topple.
To be simple is not simply easy
In others' pain when you are busy
Truly enough to say you are crazy
Let your path be too rosy.
Man of empathy never fails in life
Never let others bear human strife
Everywhere he can boldly stand
Graced is he to understand.

66. ROSE

Resplendent flower of miracles
Oasis in the desert of hatred
Sweeps away the filth of obstacles
Emblem of love wholly sacred.
Evergreen, everlasting bridge of love
Serene, sober and tender hub
Oscillating in the swing of pleasure
Reciprocates love of lovers as measure.
Breathing amidst thorns of bitterness
Dreaming daily to spread happiness
Sticking the broken hearts of sacredness
Destined to die in solitariness.
Not just a flower to show radiant glow
Not just colorful to allure fellows
More than a flower to say a lot
Being a lover fortunate his lot.
Metaphor and simile for the poet
Hope for the lover and the beloved
Ladder to the love eternal
Lovely is its internal and external.

67. THOU ARE MY BEAUTY

The rose among the flowers
The moon among the stars
My love my beauty thou are
Before you unwanted all are
You are my valentine
I am at cloud nine
Our love more divine
Like honey more pristine.
Everyday a valentine day
When you wish to stay
None can make me go astray
For our love let me pray.
Thou are my real beauty
Amidst worldwide celebrity.

68. PANACEA

Love is panacea to all social evils
Vanquishes unsocial devils
Amidst failure and success
Life to live with caress.
Labour is panacea to health
As health is wealth
Exercise keeps body fit before death
Reading is panacea to mind
Mind grabs the whole mankind
Leaving some usefull behind.

69. HARDTIME

The flowers of hard time bloom in the garden of adversity
Pervades the fragrance of sweetness beyond society
Lucky are those who heartily embrace
From heaven does shower the stream of eternal grace.
Hard time comes to one and all
To test courage and stamina
It gives a great lesson to the world
How to and where to survive
Amidst all rises and falls
But one thing is sure to say
For a long period it can never stay.
However painfull hard time is
It always makes life joyful
Taking away the current of sarrows
Again makes life peaceful.

70. FIGHT FOR

Fighting for myself for what I am doing wrong or right
If am right I can right the wrong with might
Love, peace, harmony and unity, integrity
Can only sustain humanity and fight for solidarity.
Fight for own self wins the race
Fight for other to defeat your self
To balance the creation of Almighty
Which gives you th power of divinity.
Fight for the best to out the worst
The best will be in at any cost
That offers identity with integrity
When you are the worshiper of humanity.

71. SEASONS

All seasons the amalgam of human life
No luxury possible without strife
Existence of life lies in each season
Enriches with the sources of various reasons.
Every seasons is meaningful
However, some are painfull
Alltogether they make life joyful
Must we no how they purposfull.
For each and every life in rise and fall
Teaches the mankind how to adjust
In every situation the best or the worst.

72. SERENITY

Booster of life to calm down five senses
Opens the gate of success
Panacea to all mental evils
The best weapon to drive away social devils.
Serenity of mind gives creativity
Serenity of place provides peace and equanimity
Serenity of action brings solutions
Driving away all hallucinations
Serenity of words draws one's attraction.

73. SELF CONFIDENCE

Self confidence my strength to face any challenge
Makes me stand before the huddles to embrace
All adversity opens the gate to take the privilege
Blessed I am to handle the problems with god's grace.
Opens the gates of success with full confirmation
Strengthening the background of destination
And also increases the power of concentration
And a sophisticated technique to win all competition.

74. MISTAKES

Mistakes are potions for enrichment
Opportunity for refinement
Revision for rectification
Lead us to perfection.
like a teacher teaches
Like a preacher preches
Opening the storehouse of riches
The disparity and distance it bridges.
Mistakes are common for humans
For their longlife achievment
Hence one should not treat common.

75. LOVE BOND

A bridge of magnate nobody can splinter
Made in heaven by the Almighty creator
Divinely moulded and shaped to reinforce
All adversities of the world, of course.
It can join, break and rejoin again
If well understood in communion
When pleasure replaced by pain
No power in the world can ban.

76. CONFLICT

• 78 •

Conflict the result of misunderstanding
Lack of understanding provokes heinous conflict
Endurance and compromise captivates
The power of conflict.
Sometimes conflict is a must
Without which nothing be sought
However, it may hurt
Solution open if you are caught.
Sometimes it ruins before
We reach the target of life
Stops the progress of mind
When no time to stand for mankind.

77. CONNECTED

Connected are we for a divine purpose
Something lying blank be filled with
To offer a gift for solidarity
Abide by the direction of the Almighty.
Connected are parents and offsprings
Bride and bridegrom, heart and soul
For they render something meaningfull
Helping growth and development insightfull.
Connected to something or somebody
Might create a mighty bridge of affection
In between the two poles of overlong distance
To fulfill the self of both sides.

78. BRIDGE

Build a bridge of love to meet each other
Closely to know one another
To understand you and all with divine bliss
Sharing and caring the base of life's edifice.
Build a bridge of relation unhurt
Passing the message of unity
Slogans of equality and fraternity
Accomplishing the purpose of the Almighty.
Bridge between teachers and students
Explore the land of knowledge and wisdom
Fertilizing with the manure of culture
To harvest crops of lore and rapture.

79. BETTER LATE THAN NEVER

Late is precious, valuable and meaningfull
Not always dangerous and harmfull
Hurried life hurriedly passes away
Unless we keep in our own way.
To delay is not action of intention
Rather a chance to revise action
Action in a haste goes waste
But late never ruins the rest.
Hence beter late than never
Keep in mind forever.

80. TRANSLATION DAY

Life is an imitation, a recreation
A translation of some good action
May be a better creation than earlier
No matter retold here and there.
The best way of language acquisition
Culture, customs, habits and humanisation
From one generation to other generation
Invention and exploration of communication.
Means of knowing others in details
Can enrich our mind without fail
The more we read more we translate
The more we translate more we inculcate
Profound wisdom of great mind
Before we leave this beautiful mankind.

81. THE WORLD IS ONE FAMILY

We are humans from same race

Born with God's Grace

We are from the same parent

His Excellence, O, omnipresent.

The world belongs to all wherever we live

And we all belongs to the same world

Where our religion is only humanity

Our duty is to work for solidarity

We are all brother and sister

The sons and daughters of the Almighty

We must follow the principles of equlity and fraternity

Living in one family the world of diversity

Still we are one in all to have unity.

82. THE REAL FIGHTER

The truthful are real fighter
Faithful competitor, fair rider
Undefeated soldier without helter-skelter
In the battlefield of society.
The honest of the real fighter
To fight against dishonesty
They never change their path of chastity
Which gives them proper identity.
The simple and the humble are the brave hearts
The can face any challenge with their guts
In their life they can never hurt
In adversity eventhough cought.

83. GANDHI THE MAHATMA

Gregarious

Ability

Nucleus

Daring

Honest

Immortal

Tolerant

Humble

Efficient

Magnanimous

Admirer

Hard worker

Adjustment

Time bound

Magnificent

Anchor

84. WORLD ANIMALS DAY

We are all animals
Some are carnival
Some are none
Both are in need
Helpful indeed.
Dependable we are
Commited to care
Daring to share
Each other free and fair
To rear and nurture.

85. OLD IS GOLD

Often told
Old is gold
Meaning many fold
Wisdom they hold
Balancing hot and cold.
The old can foretell
What to curtail
And what not.
The old are experienced
Practically full of oppulence
Over their self confidence
Can win other's credence.

86. NEVER GIVE UP

Be calm and stable
Just to be able
Never give up
Stay with hope
Time will enable.
One can fail only if quit
And becomes unfit
To survive at least
In the society of fest and feast
As no longer stays mist
However dense and deep.

87. SOCIAL MEDIA

Super spreader
Risk holder
Worldwide messenger
Of hidden things, beholder.
Life long dedicated to expose the truth
Without caring for risk of life
They can overcome huddles
Flying over the wings of honesty and integrity
They can lit the light of verity
As the servant of the society.

88. FIRST PRIZE

In life first prize
Really a matter of surprise
Inspire in disguise
Hope, trust maximize.
To be first is not easy
To be easy is not crazy
Anybody can be the first
To have the prize at last
But nothing happens fast
What we need to secure
Practice in regularity can ensure
Which gradually makes us mature
To taste the sweetness of what we capture
The end is his or her to rapture.

89. WORLD POST DAY

Selfless servant
Employed permanent
By central government
Wondrous achievement.
The world post day
A day to celebrate to give away
The message of service and generesity
It Closes the distance
In between two places
Carrying the bags of letters and parcels
From place to place and person to person
Through out the year of all seasons.

90. GIRLS ARE JEWELS

Hidden powers
Blooming flowers
Need of the hours
Let them empower.
As polite as water
As pure as air
Blowing everywhere
Without discrimination
With no malafide intention
Let them accept and honour
For their trait and nature.
Girls are as priceless as jewels
Beside us they dwell
Sparkling like a diamond forever.

91. LIVE TO GROW

life is living
Live life to grow
Let it move and fly
As birds high in the sky.
Life is aging
Passing through ages
Years after years in phases
Innocency to maturity
And maturity to motality
Sometimes somewhere
Motality to inmotality.

92. DANCE THE RHYTHM OF LIFE.

Life dances when in rapture
Sings even when in torture
Often plays in competition
Mirroring all reflections.
Dance is the life
Dance is the rhythm
And song of humanity
Consoles the depressed souls
Convinces the diverse minds
Constitutes the slices of life
Taking away the mundane strife.
It exercises is part of life
Touching every corner
Promises to shapes destiny.

93. OUR ACTIONS ARE OUR FUTURE

Life is full of action and reactions
That builds human future
Actions taken in present
Nurture our future
Today prepares a stage
For future coverage
What is done today
Preserves for tomorrow
Good actions gives good results
And bad action bad results
So to say action decides future
If the present is dark, future will be dark
Needles to say it is common to mark.

94. TRAIN YOUR MIND STRONGER

Stronger mind

Captures wind

Out of depth

Printed till death.

Train your mind

Stronger its behind

Human have a speciality

Having a unique mind of positivity.

Positive mind results surity in success

When fear may flee away

And negative mind negative results in excess.

95. DO GOOD, GOOD WILL COME TO YOU

You will get what you give
Nothing to give nothing to receive
Life is to share
Everything will care.
Do good for others
Other will do good for you
Think good for others
Other will think good for you.
Mutual action brings cooperation
Coperation leads to gratification
Purposeful actions always purposeful
And harmful actions always harmful.
Do good good will come to you
if you do bad, bad will come to you too.

96. EYES TELL WHAT WORDS CANNOT

Eyes are the silent speaker

Untold stories tellers

Speaks a lots as if a narrator

A marvelous orator.

Each symphony of human feelings-

Love, hatred, anger, sympathy

Expresed lucidly and vividy.

It catches the photograph of what it sees

And present before the mass lookers

As if stands before the beholders

Mirroring the image of everything.

Not only sees the things before it

But also reads the foibles of a character

Being an eyewitness.

97. CHOOSE WHAT CHOOSES YOU

Avoid not what comes to you

Repent not what goes from you

Choose not what or whom you love

Choose what or who loves you much.

One who loves you understands you too

He or she can never betray or go astray

But the one who does not like you

Or whom you like the most

May slip or flee away leaving you to the rest.

So nothing to be done in haste

Must we train our mind to calm down

To save the best from the worst.

98. HOPE

Hope is light to show the path of life
The whole world exists on hope
Courage and stamina it does hold
Washes away the filth of negative germs like soap.
Hope is the only thing to keep on
Efforts and journey, the ship of life to run
It only makes life move and grow
Surpassing the clouds of adversity
Twinkling admist the dark of calamity
To enlighten the world of humanity.
It is fuel to life in order to survive
Life without hope is like life without heart.

99. PEACE IN YOUR HAND

Let your hand be solemn

Humans we are to be humane

Thou are the source of peace

Strive to look at within the divine bliss.

You are the reason of your action

Your action can change the course of reaction.

You are you to stop the bad action

In return to get gratification.

Peace is in our hand to make life peacefull

The way we follow takes us to the goal mirthful

It is you who can hervest what you invest

Loss and gain just like to sides of a coin

In the absence of one the other loses identity

Thus you are the head and you are tail

You are all in one and one in all.

100. MOONLIGHTING

Silvery light enlivens the hearts of children
Mother's lullaby with the visage of moon
Bounces her to enthusiastically croon
Under the canopy of moonlight plays hide and seek.
Simile and metaphor incorporated in moonlight
Like the affulgent hues of rainbow highly delight
Sometimes somewhere a stream of divine love and peace
That showers upon the head of the mighty God
Often a ray of hope to heal the wound bloming one's lot
Angel of serenity turns up to tranqulize and mesmerize
The soul of the depressed and the oppressed to sensetize
Both words and thoughts, actions and reactions to humanize.

101. JOYOUS MOMENT

• 103 •

Joyous am I when humans show integrity
In love, duty and relationship with serendipity
Forget and forgive those erring a little mistake for universal betterment
Striving for sustaining peace, harmony and humanity with commitment.
Motherhood a joyous moment of a lady as a mother
When a sister is blessed with safety and security by a brother.
When a son or a daughter surpasses own father
That is the repture that captures together.
In reality a jayous moment.

102. REAL IS RARE

Real is rare, unreal bare

Real is fair, unreal unfair

Real is silence, unreal noise

Real is light, unreal unseen guys

Real is construction, unreal destruction.

Sometimes reality is bitter

To accept the better

That really matters

And makes the difference

In between the real and the unreal.

Sometimes reality hides

In the eyes of the beholders

Which differentiates a lot.

103. WHAT YOU DO COME TO YOU

Today's dark is tomorrow's light
No good to fight for might
Someone's wrong is other's right
My right is yours wrong to cite.
One's mentality begets the results
Whether it is bad of good
The way we look decides
Shades of life in various moods.
We humans are men of actions.
Every action has reactions
Some worthy and some unworthy
But we must harvest what we invest
Thus better to do the best
Among all without any waste.

104. THE BEST PEOPLE COME UNEXPECTEDLY

Like the downpour of rains
Fruits of labour always remain
Every pain has gain
How can the best refrain
From the Almighty's summon.
No people are good or bad
They become what they have already done
The truth is that the best of all
Never comes one day at all
It takes time to rise and fall
The best people appear unexpectedly
Nobody can defy inadvertently.

105. LISTEN TO YOURSELF

Listen to yourself before you speak
Speak to yourself before you skip
Fly to the sky before your fall
Everything in you, you are all in all.
Listening widens the domain of acceptance
To explore the land of perseverance
With patience and confidence
Preserves the good in opulence
For the world's benevolence.
Listen to yourself gathers courage
Everywhere everytime does encourage
To do things with perfect knowledge.

106. WHAT WE DO IS BEAUTY OF LOVE

We must do what we love
And we must love what we do
Actions with love crests the destination
Love for actions make you rich in possessions.
Out of love emerges the real beauty
Searching the newness in tranquility
For the benefit of humanity
That works of solidarity, equality
With the slogan of universal fraternity.
Action without love never lives long
Love without action can never sing a song.
So to say what we do in love

107. LOVE, EGO, PRIDE

Love
Love what you do
Do what you love.
Ego
End ends with sorrow
With your ego.
Pride
Flattery and coaxing hide
Your inner trend of life.

108. REAL SOURCE OF JOY

Joy never comes from heaven

Nor from the paradise mundane

Nowhere found or sold anywhere

Real source of joy the concerned person.

What makes us most happy and joyful is selfless service

A loving heart, a caring mind and sharing hand always offer bliss

You are your strength, stamina, pain and pleasure to please

Live to the fullest for the happiest life.

Living together, open heart with smiling face beget joy

Life living in generosity with no never expectations can never dismay

Life doesn't seem easy but can be made easy to display

One oneself is the cause of one's own sorrows or joy to play.

109. DREAM ENCHANTS

Dreams enchant as the monsoon
Drenched in cool wetness croon
Tender moonlit pervading soon
Grave summer hides his face at noon.
O sweet dreams for me a boon.
Every man's hunger intense
Making one and all out of tense
Life without you obviously no sense
Some say a beggar's pretence
O my fancy life's substance.
You are the friend, philosopher and guide
O wingless chariot one can ride
Taking to the valley of pride
With the flowery path to stride
Everybody's impulse standing side by side.

110. DOCTOR'S DAY

As love does not seek time to share
So do doctors, patients to take care
Thou are the angel next to the Almighty
Saviour of mankind, the worshipper of humanity.
As the wind never hesitate to touch good or bad things under the sun
So do doctors who never discriminate between convalescents high or
low
Not at all reluctant of treating and serving the victims with piss or
tools
They are the man of probity and lenience, a large hearted soul.
Hope and faith of the worst sufferer and helpless in acute ailments
They are the balm and tonic of lingering pain and diseases
What a man of serendipity and epitome of healing power!
Salute to such high personality for their incessant service to mankind.
O doctors, the light and oxygen of the passive and pensive life
Humble gratitude to your profound knowledge and wisdom
Needless to say that thou are the future of the future
Only your selfless and devoted service can rescue the kingdom.
Happy doctors day to all physicians performing as magicians
You are the symphony of life in the cacophony of human strife.